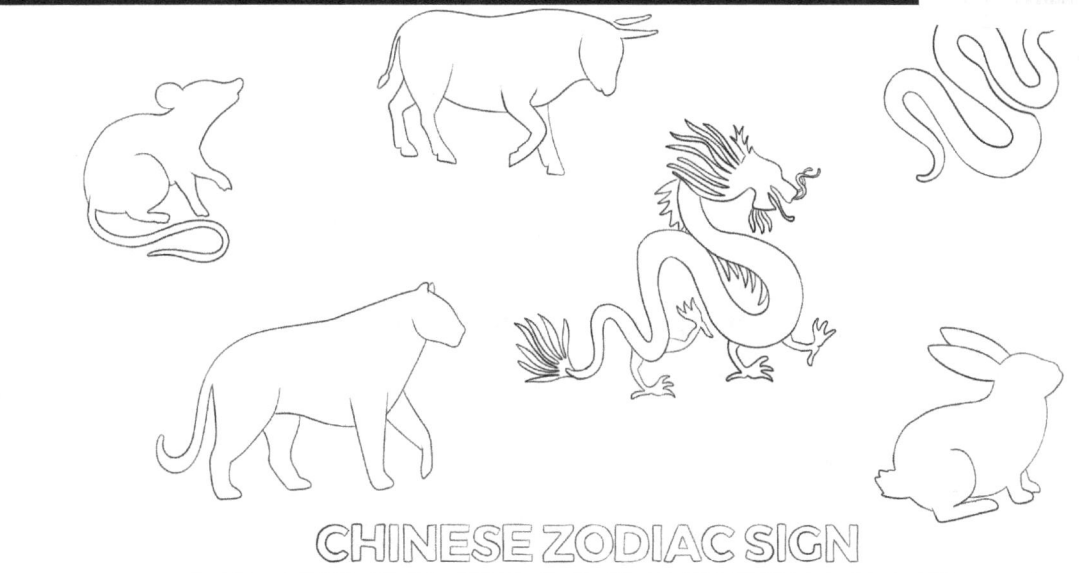

CHINESE ZODIAC SIGN

Ready to color this new adventure
Welcome to this chinese zodiac signs :

This book belongs to

....

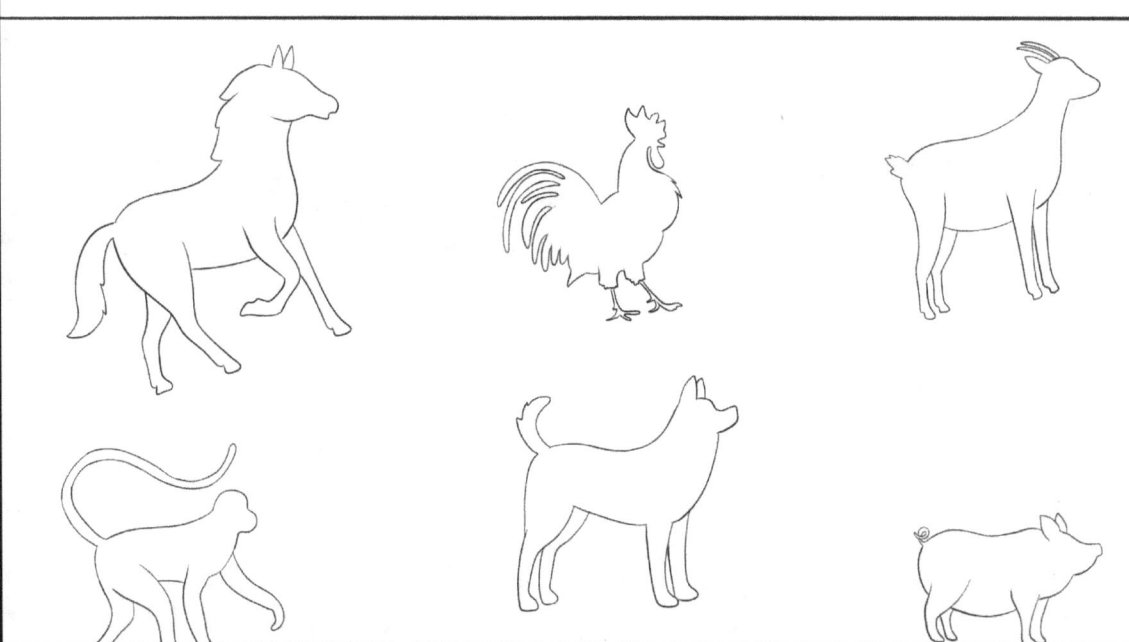

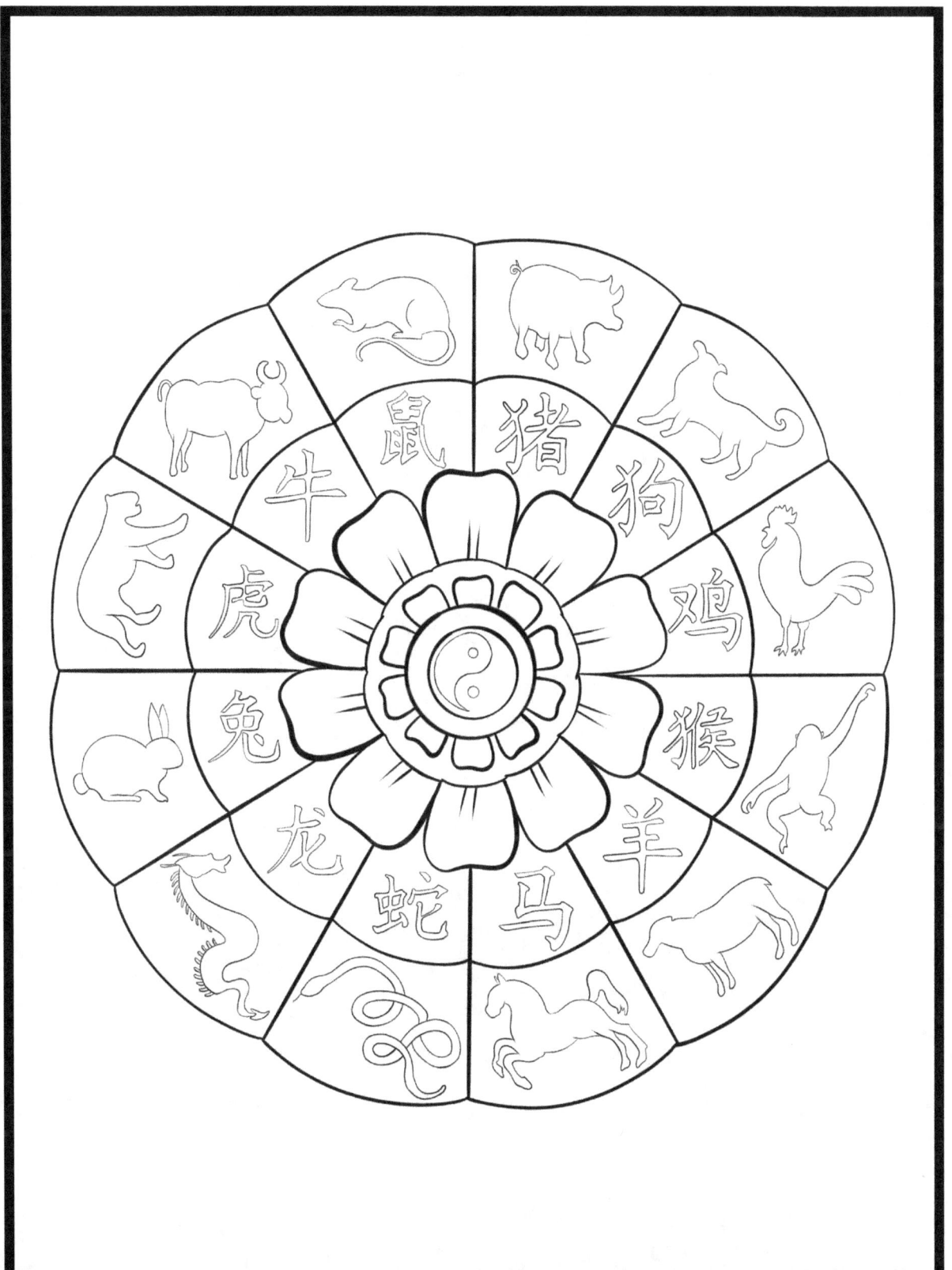

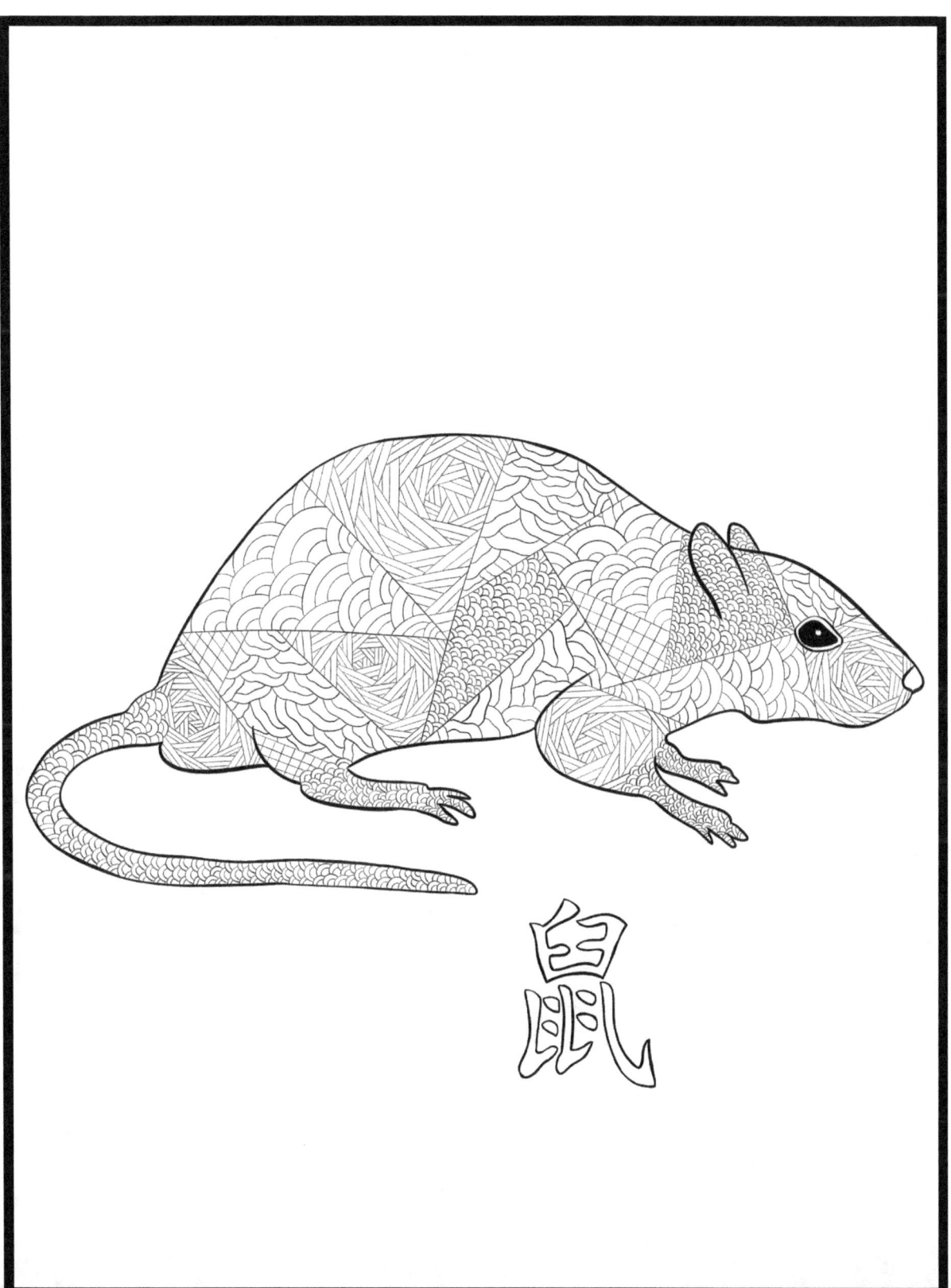

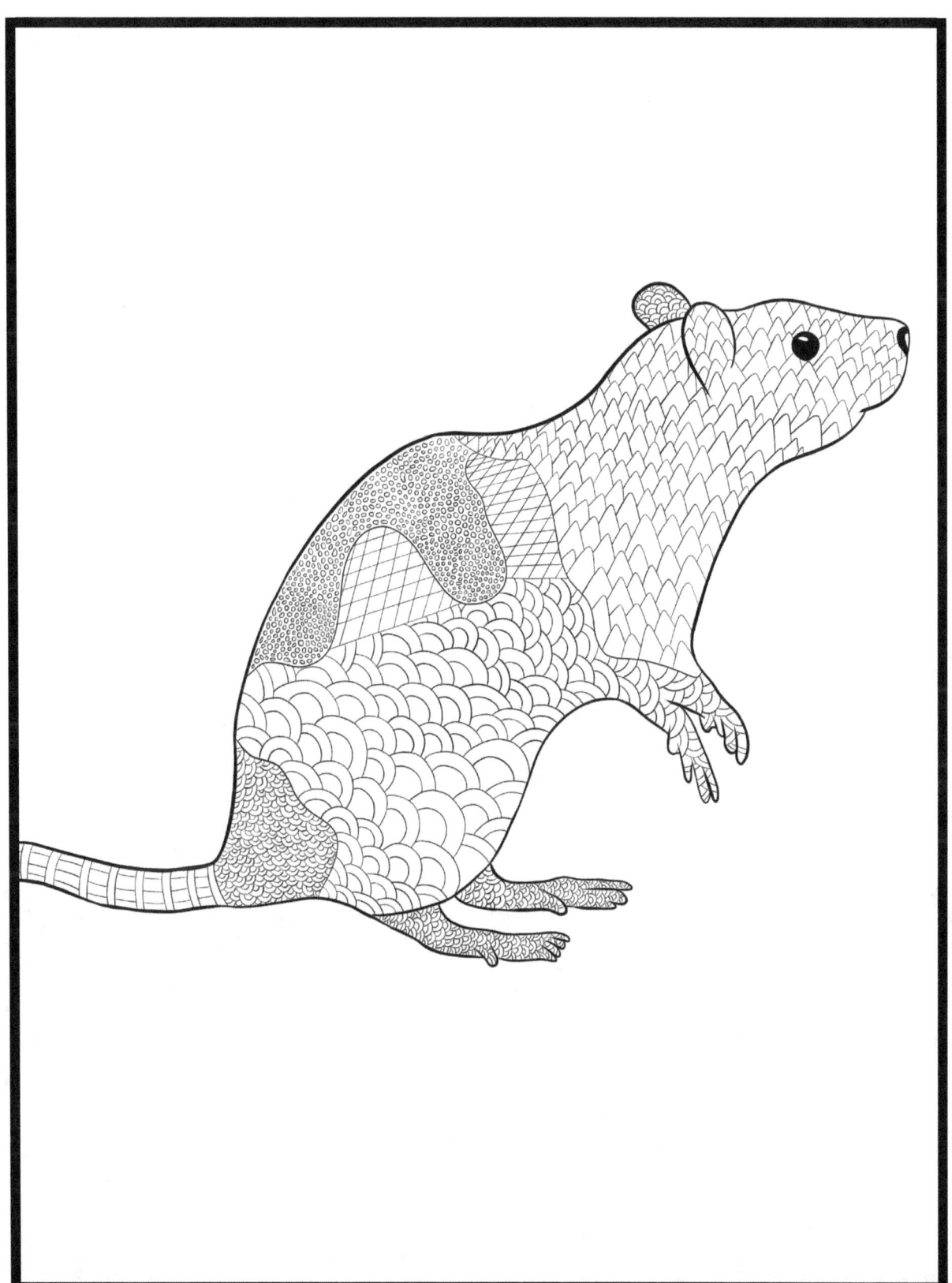

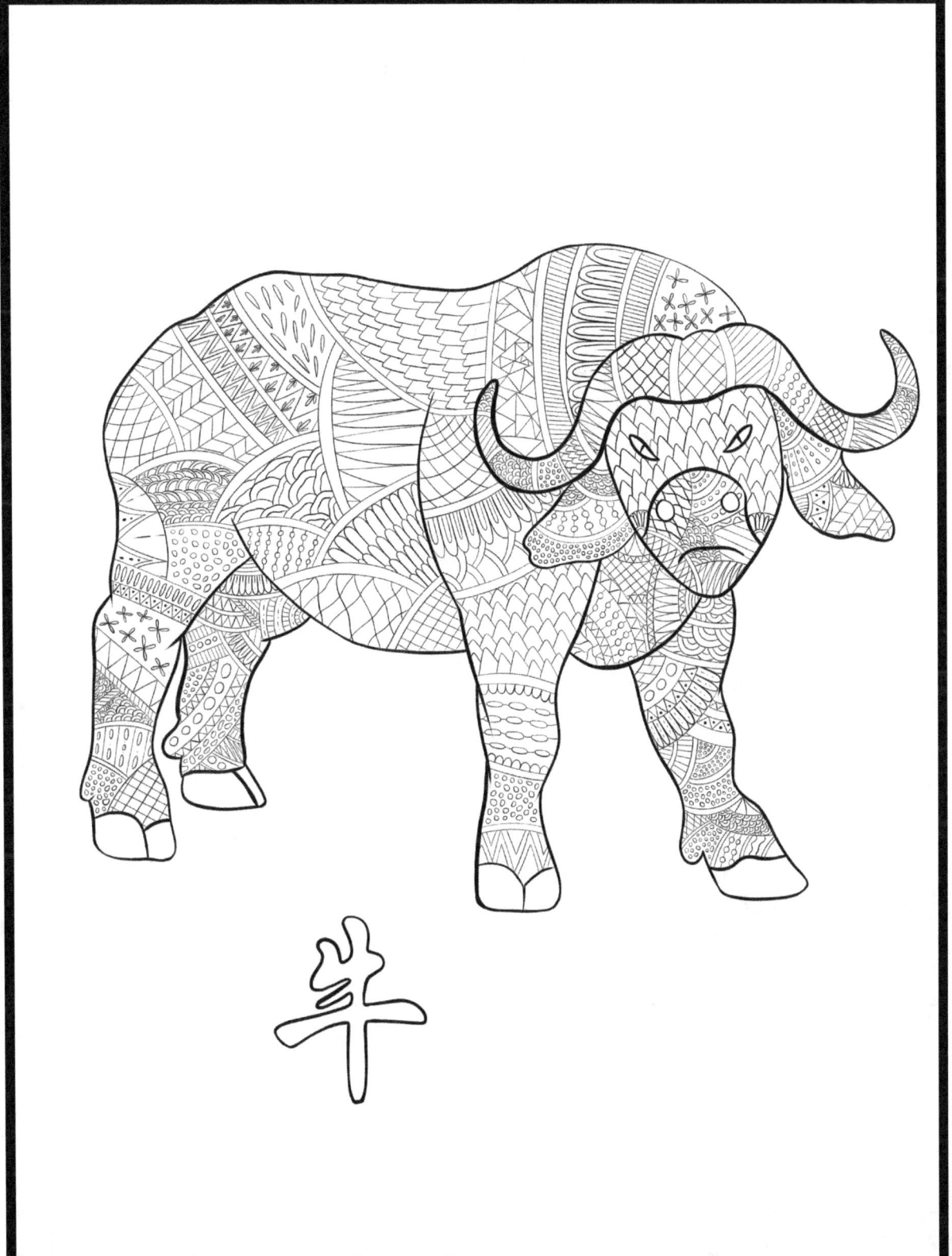

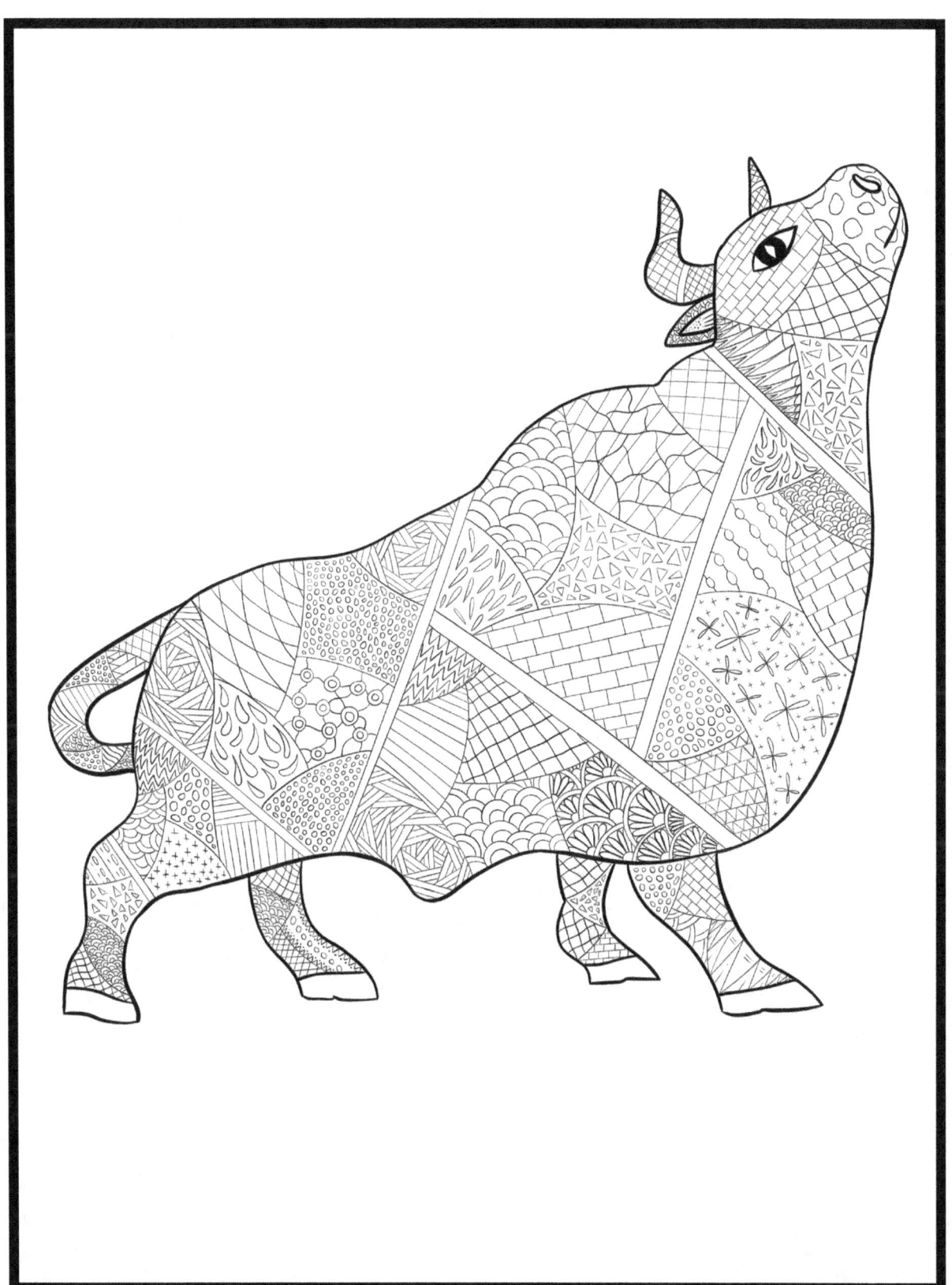

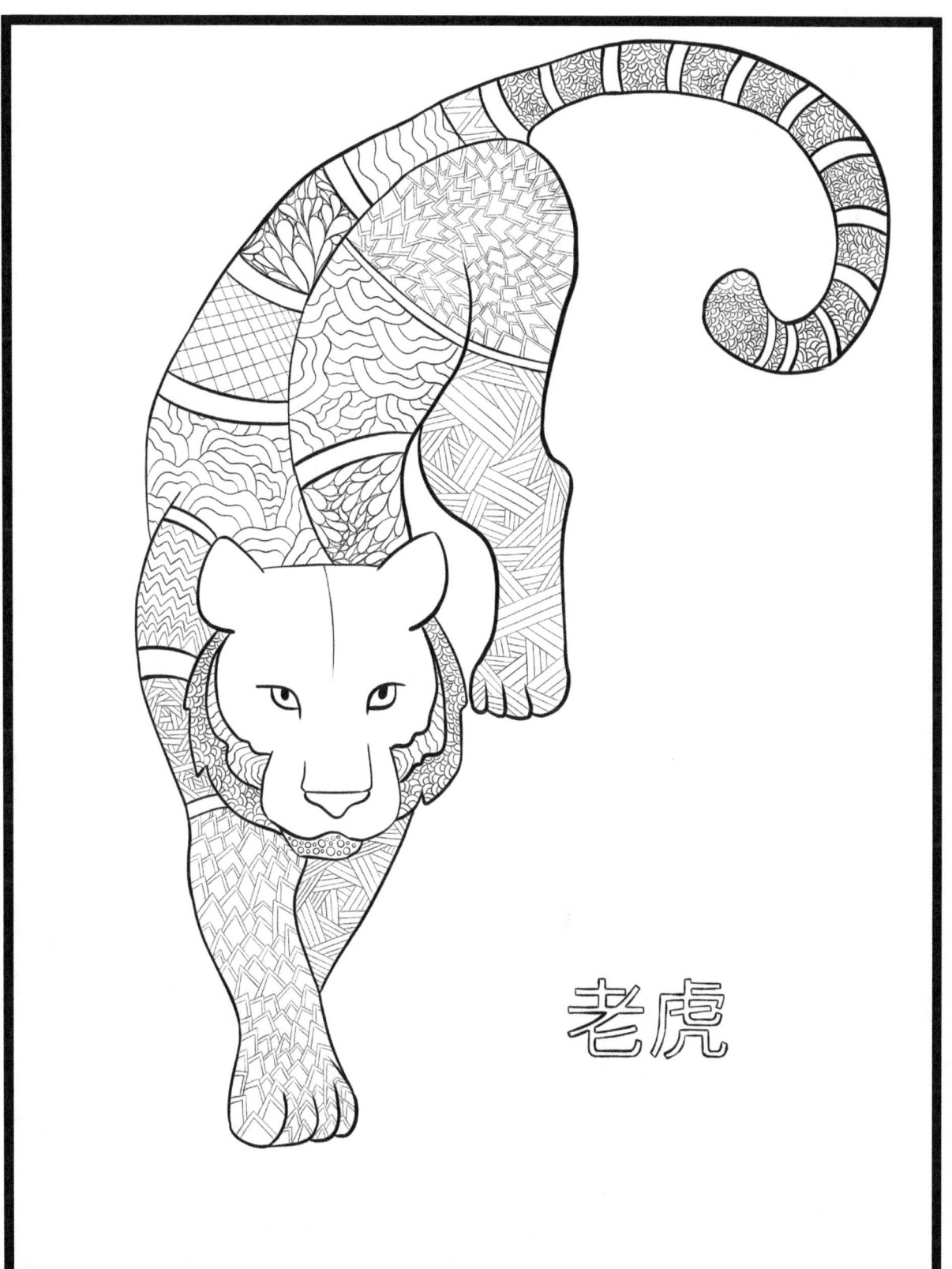

老虎

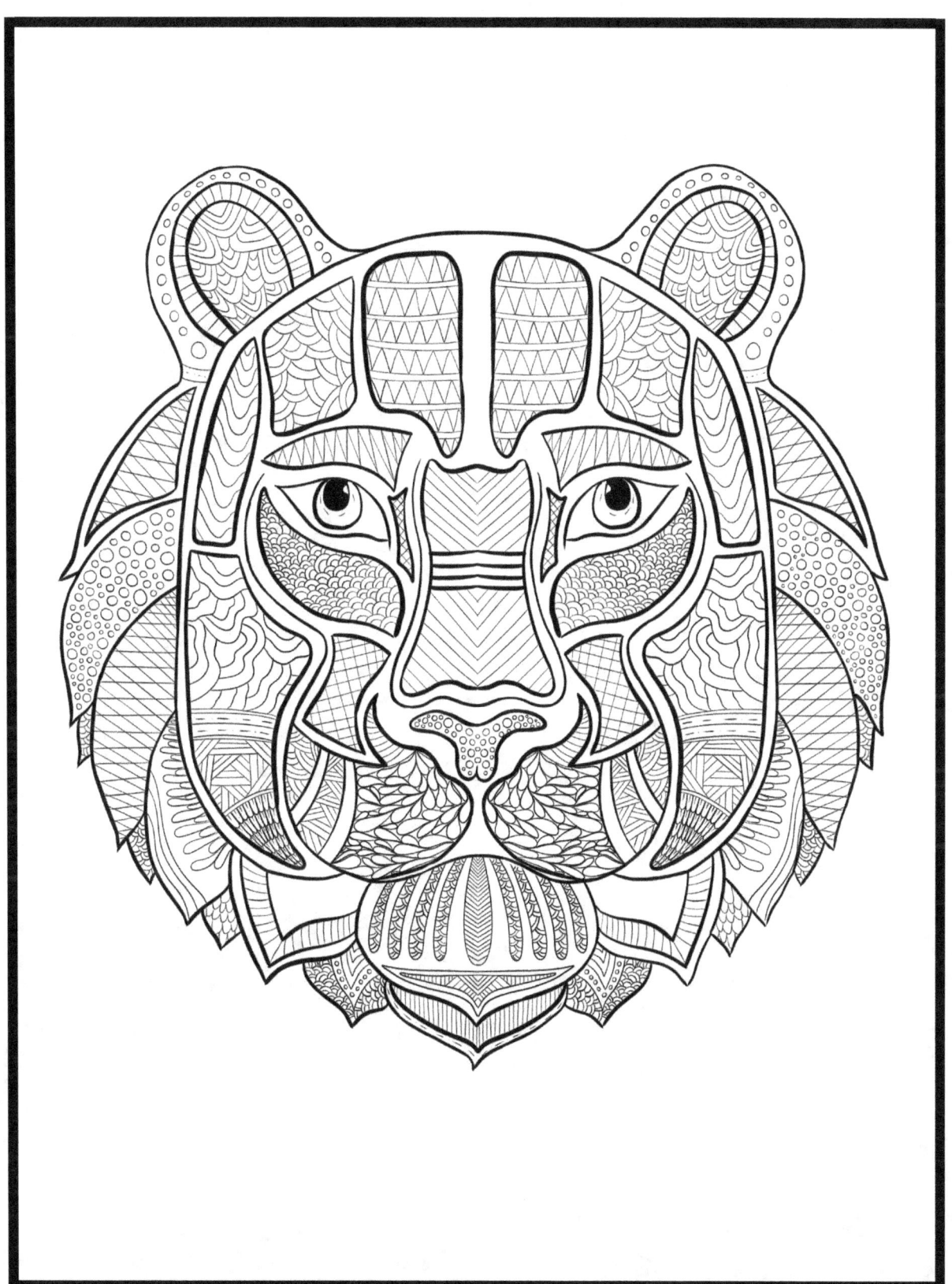

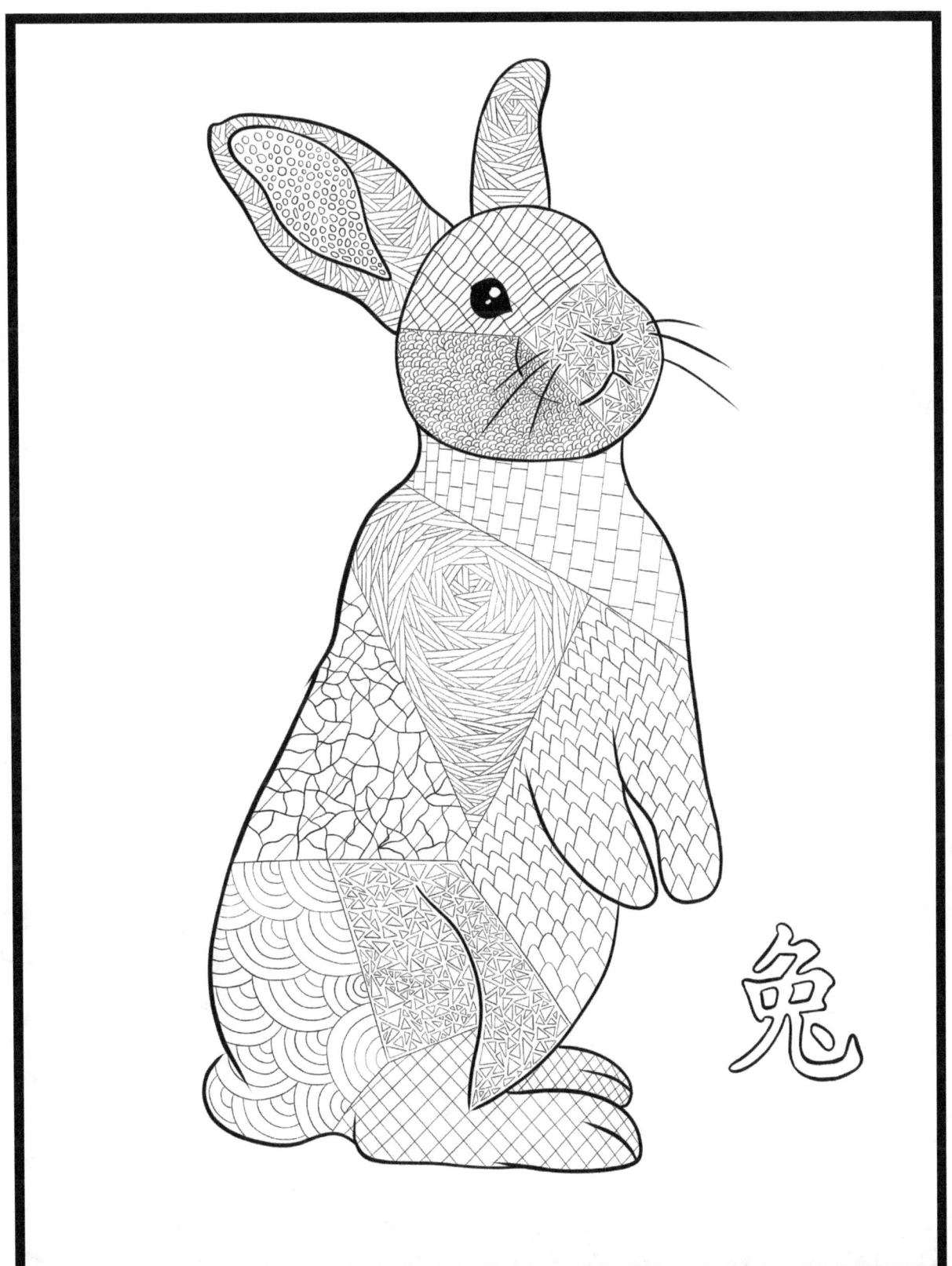

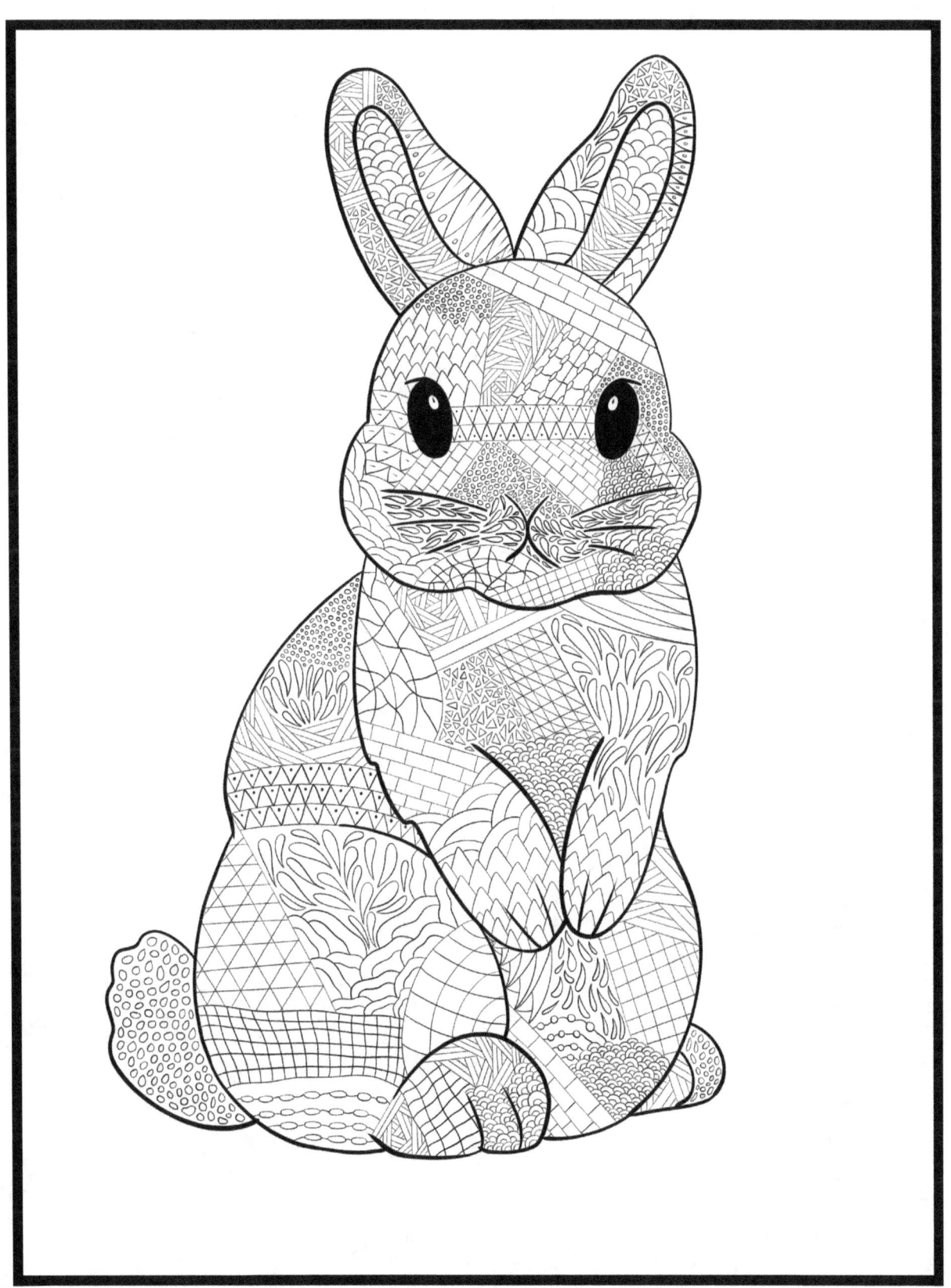

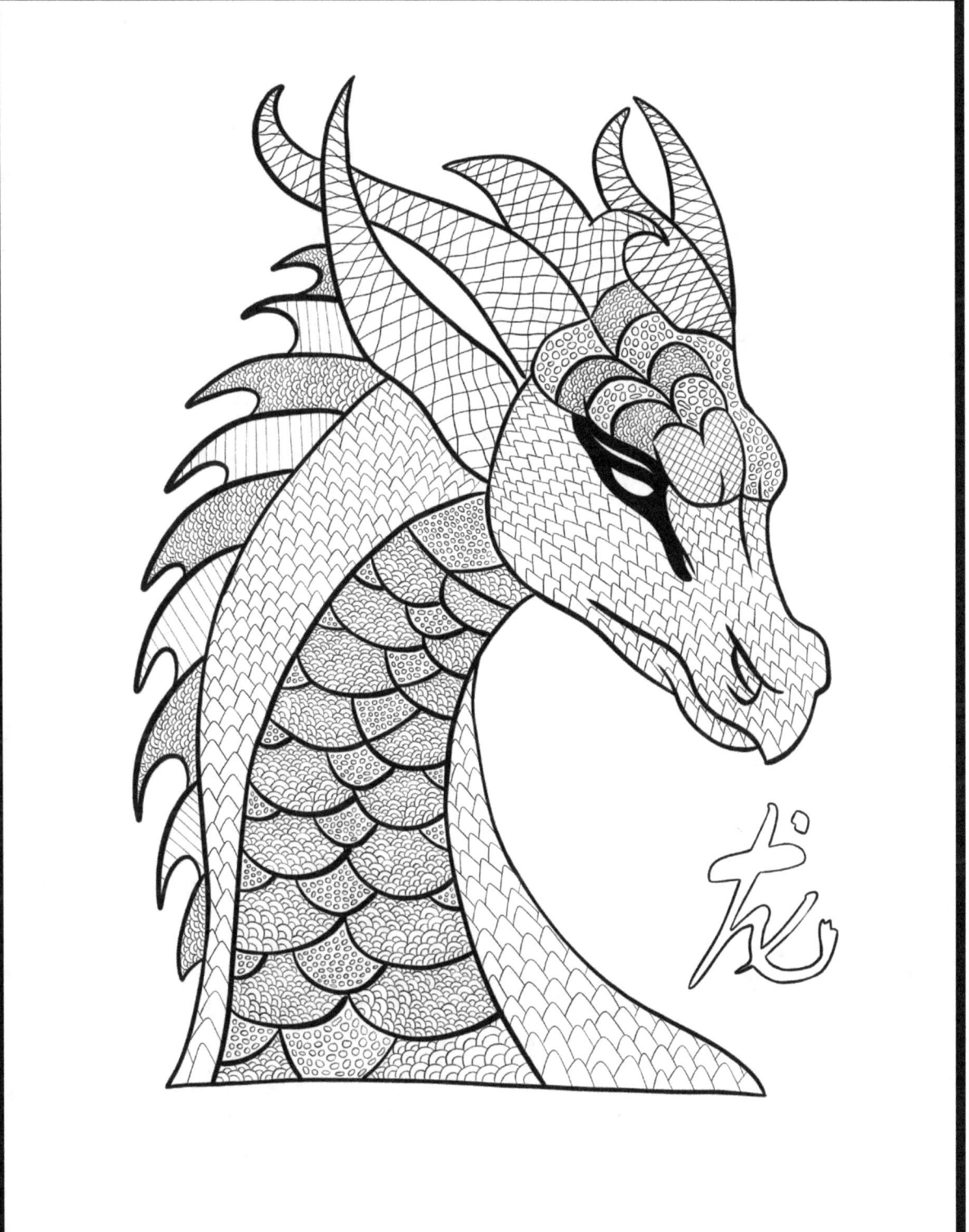

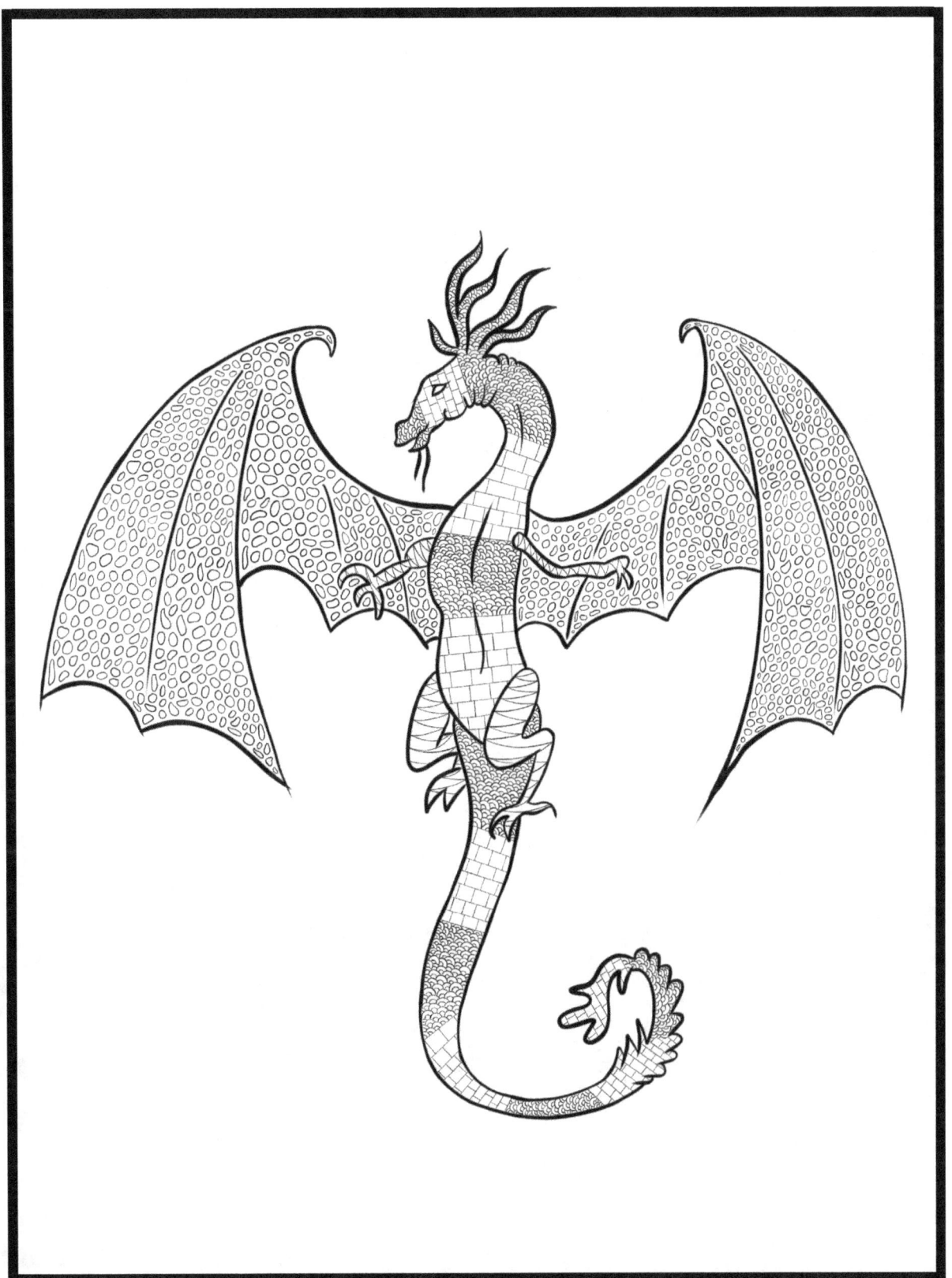

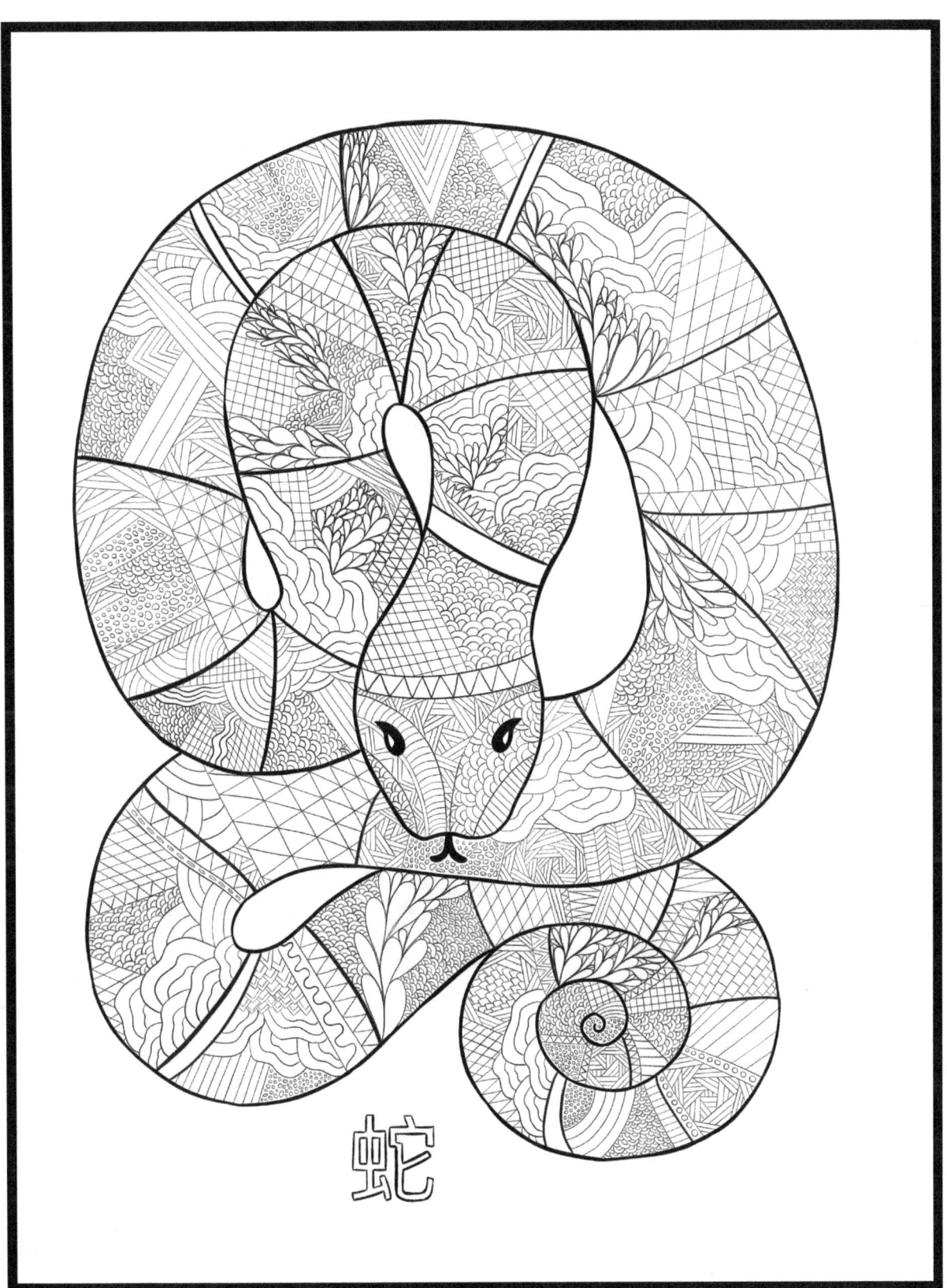

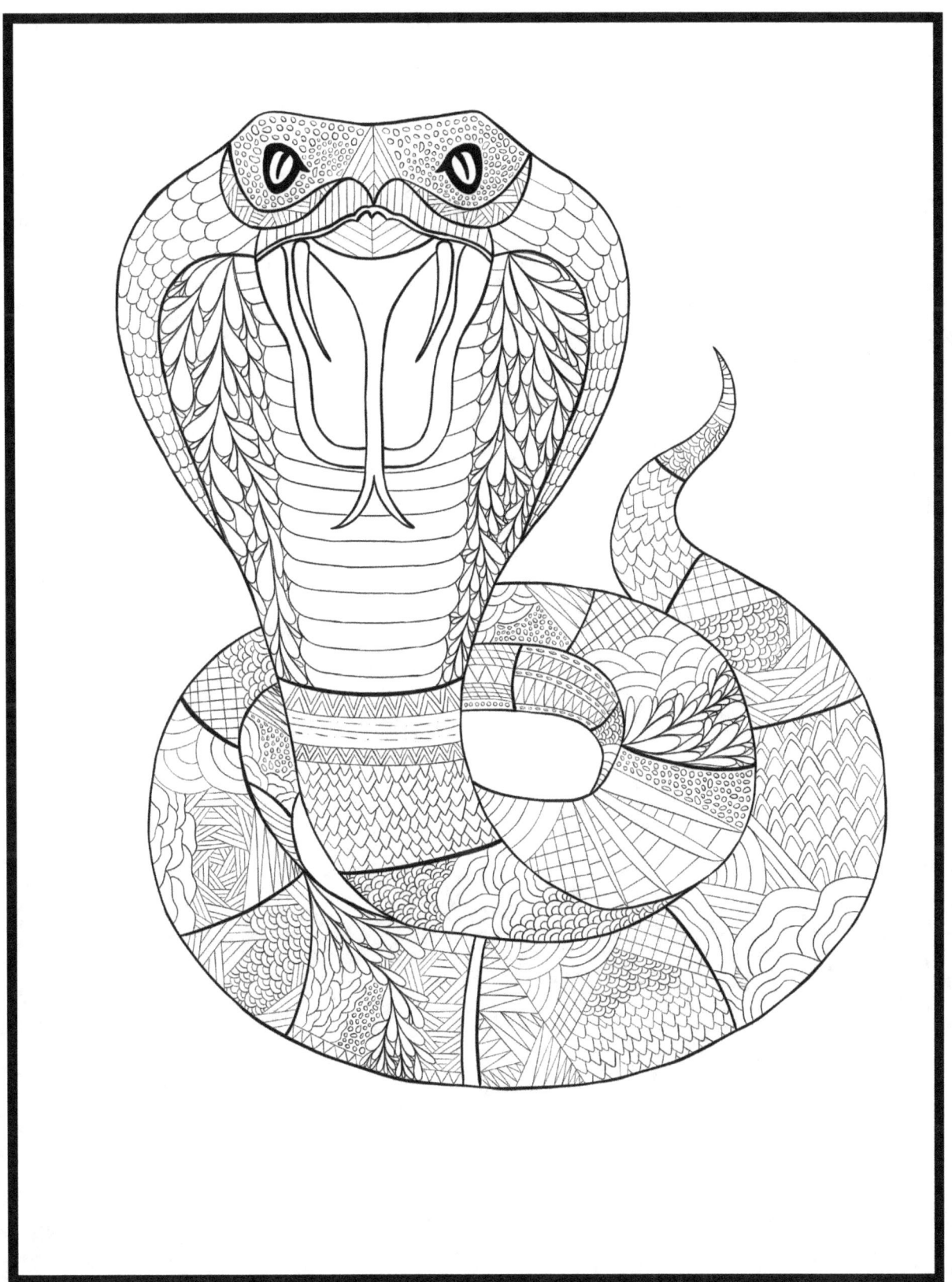

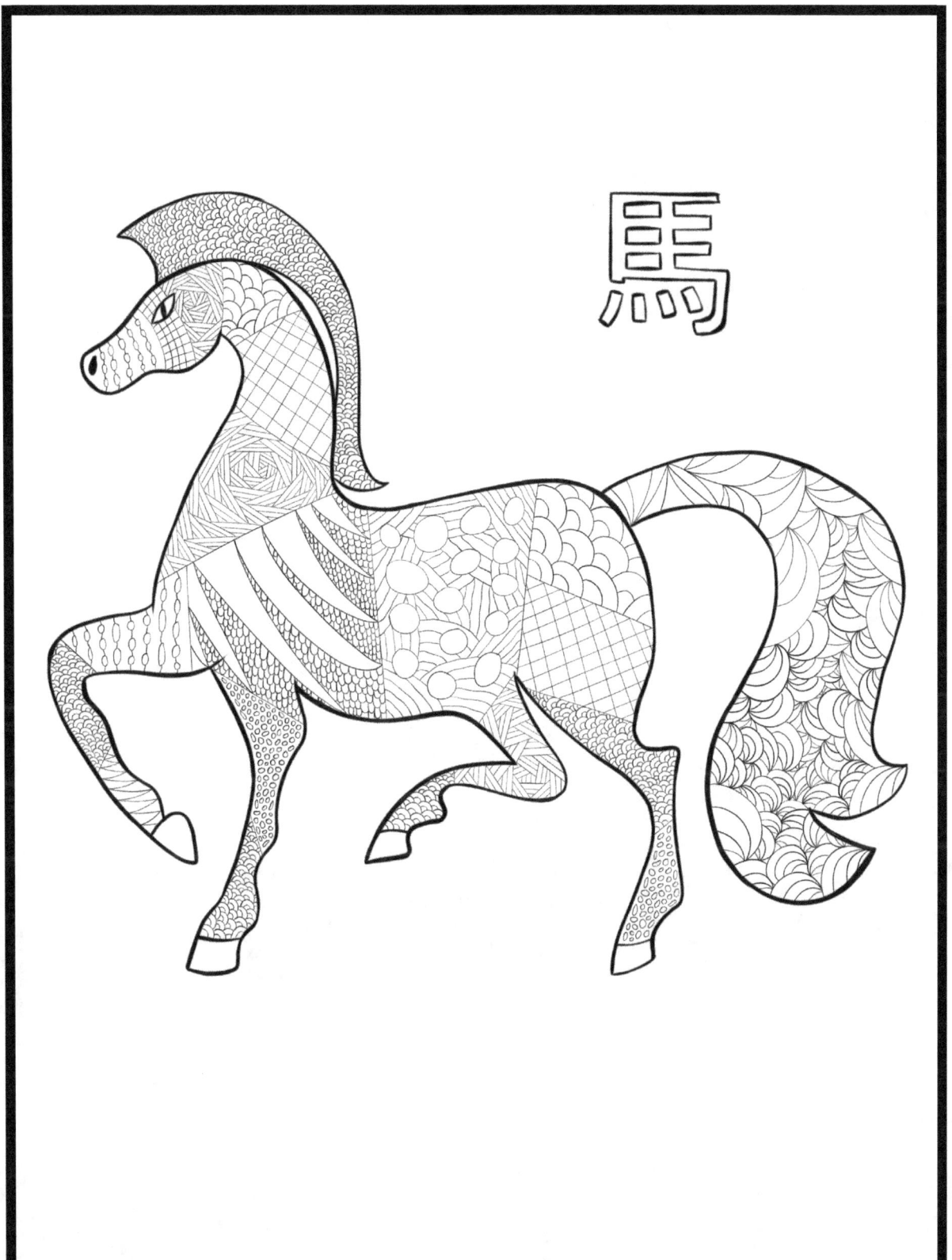

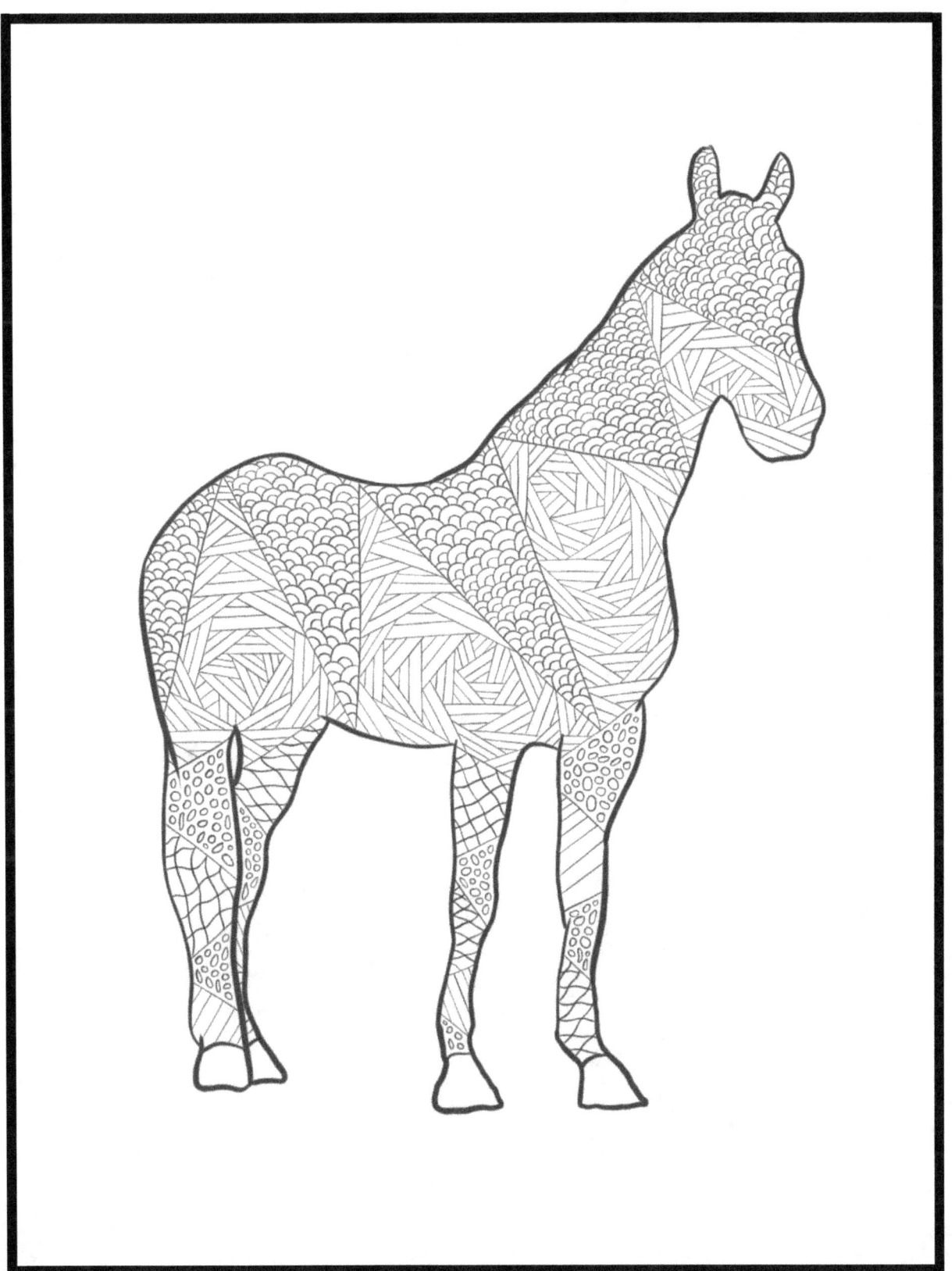

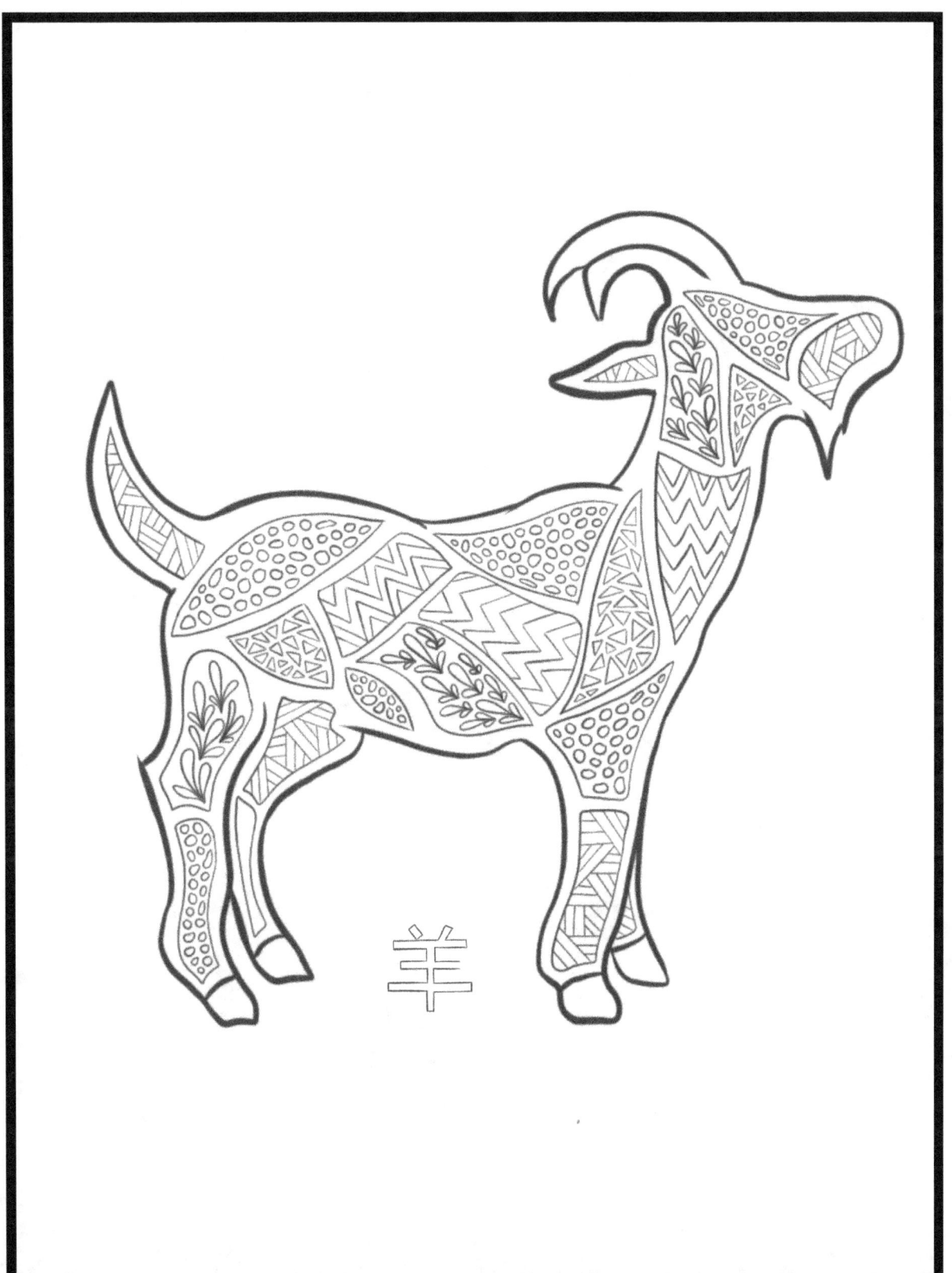

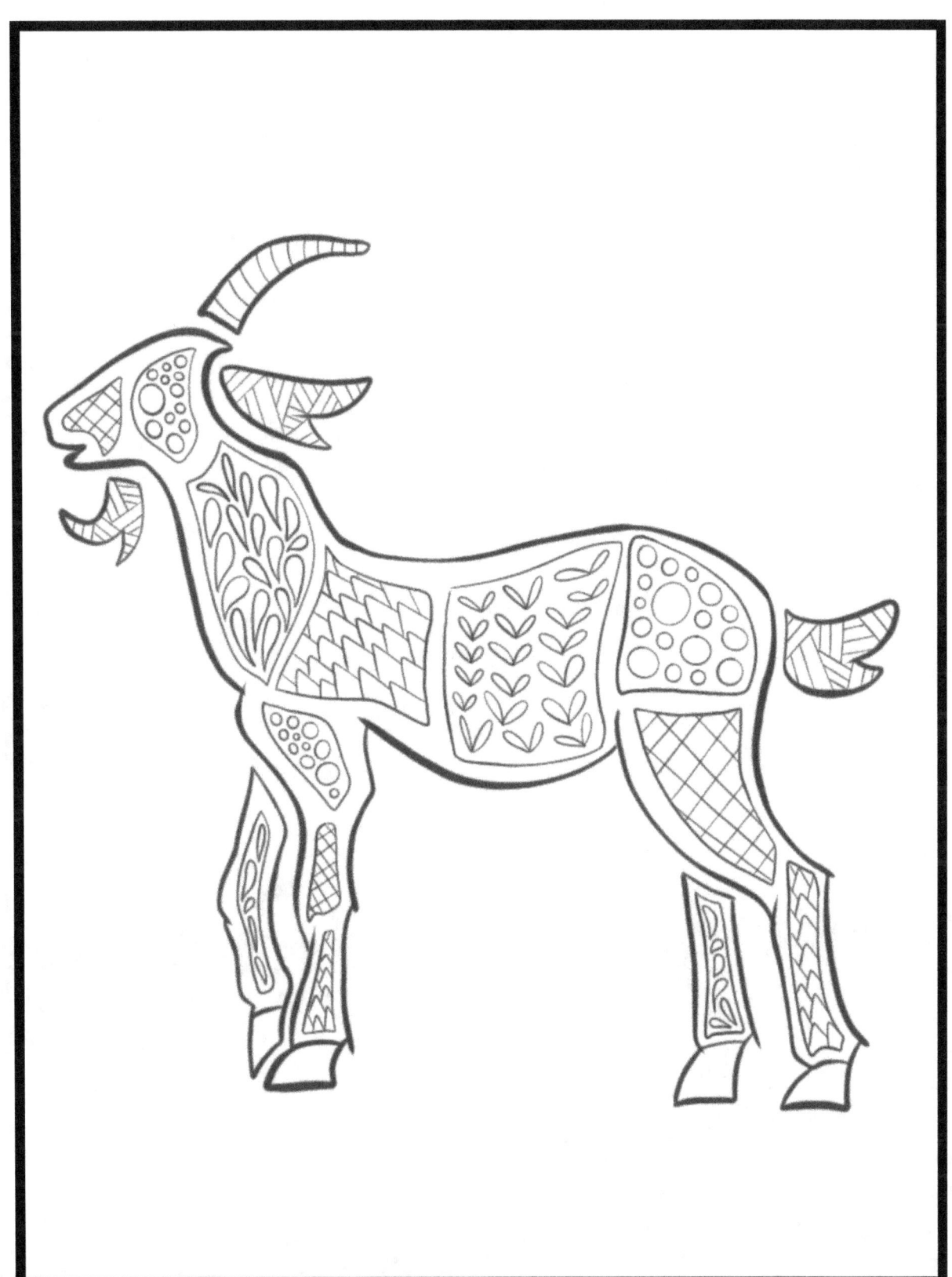

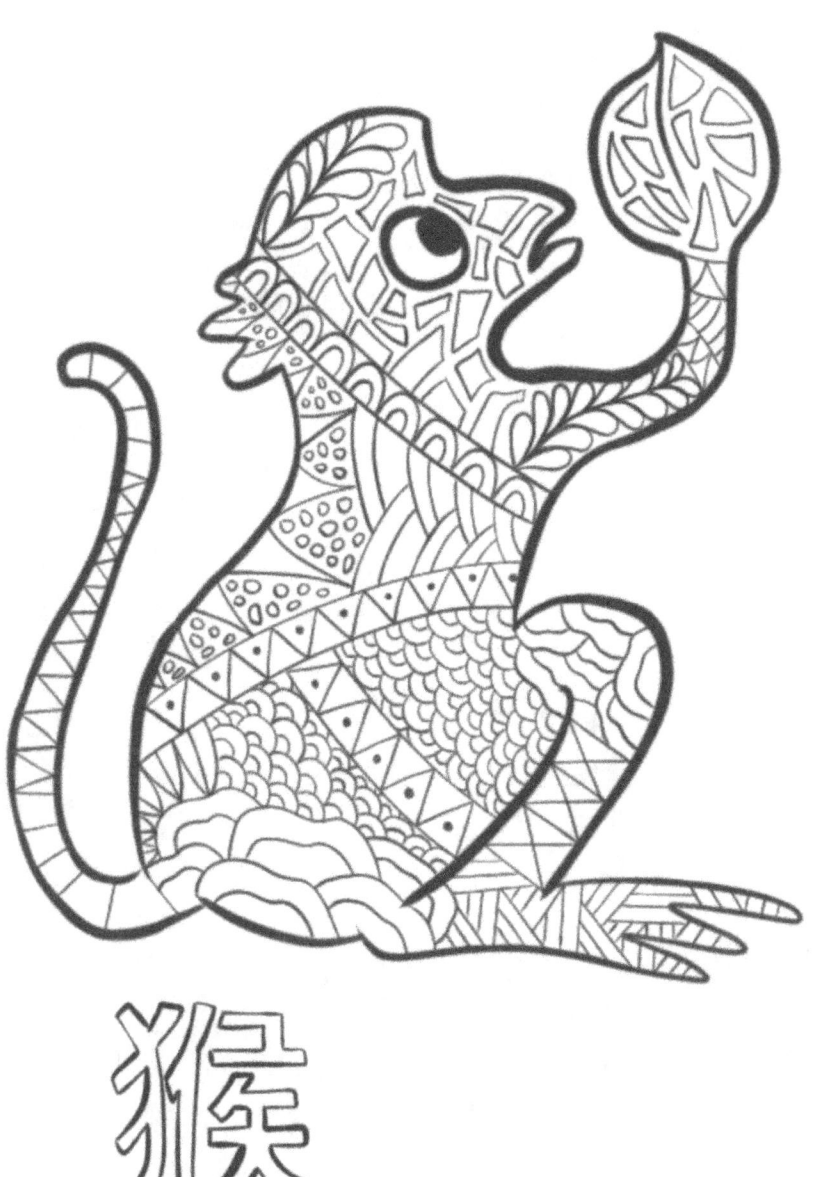

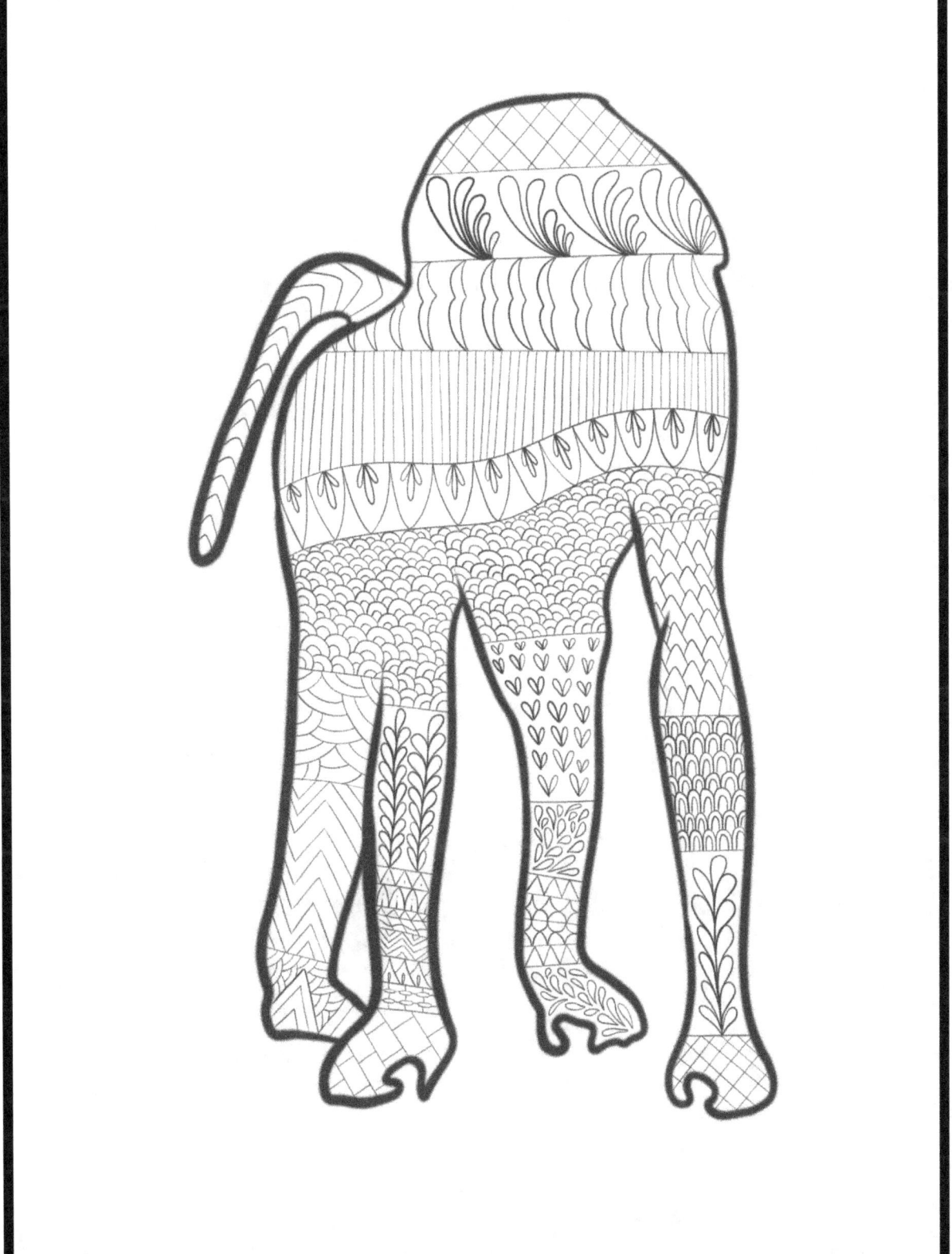

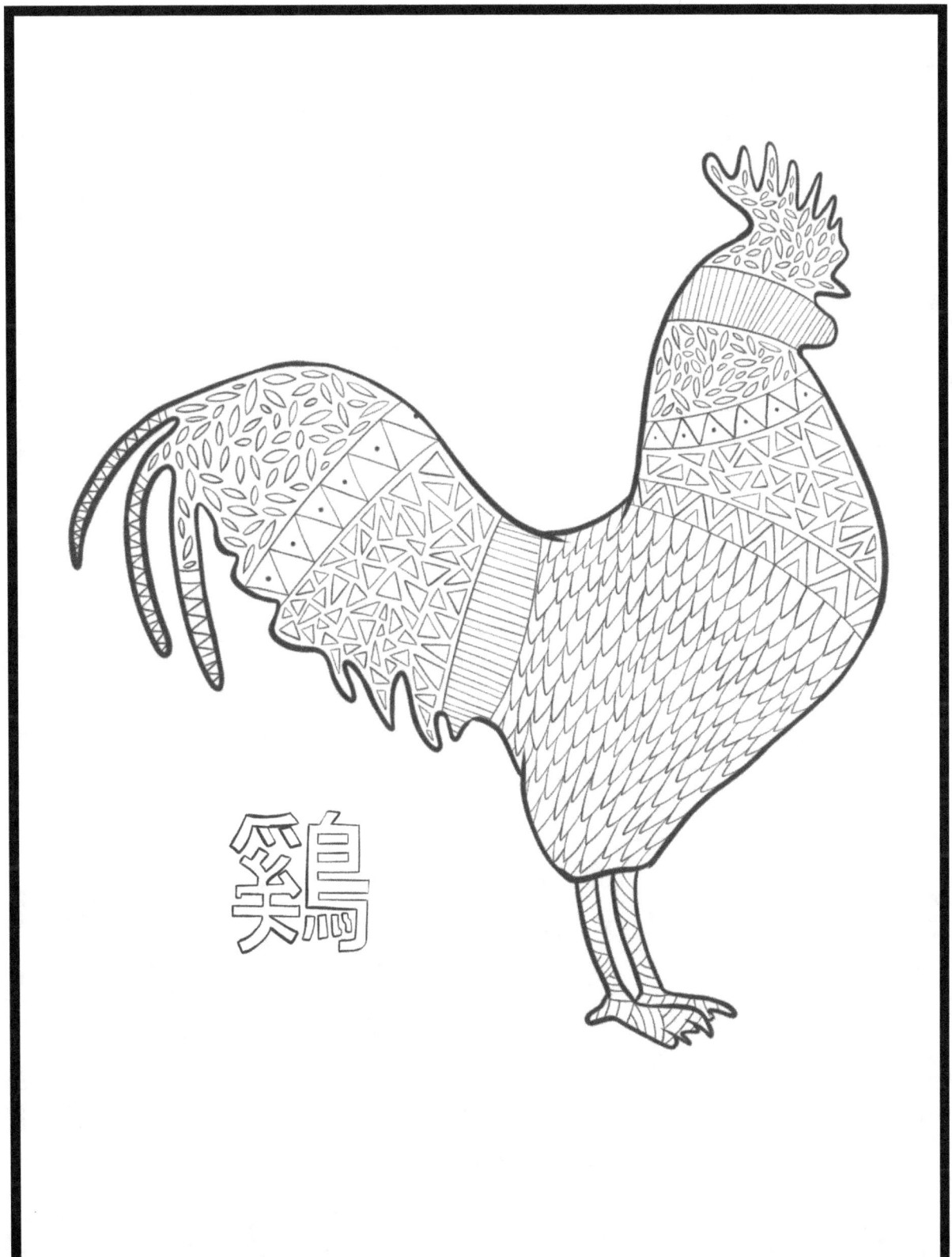

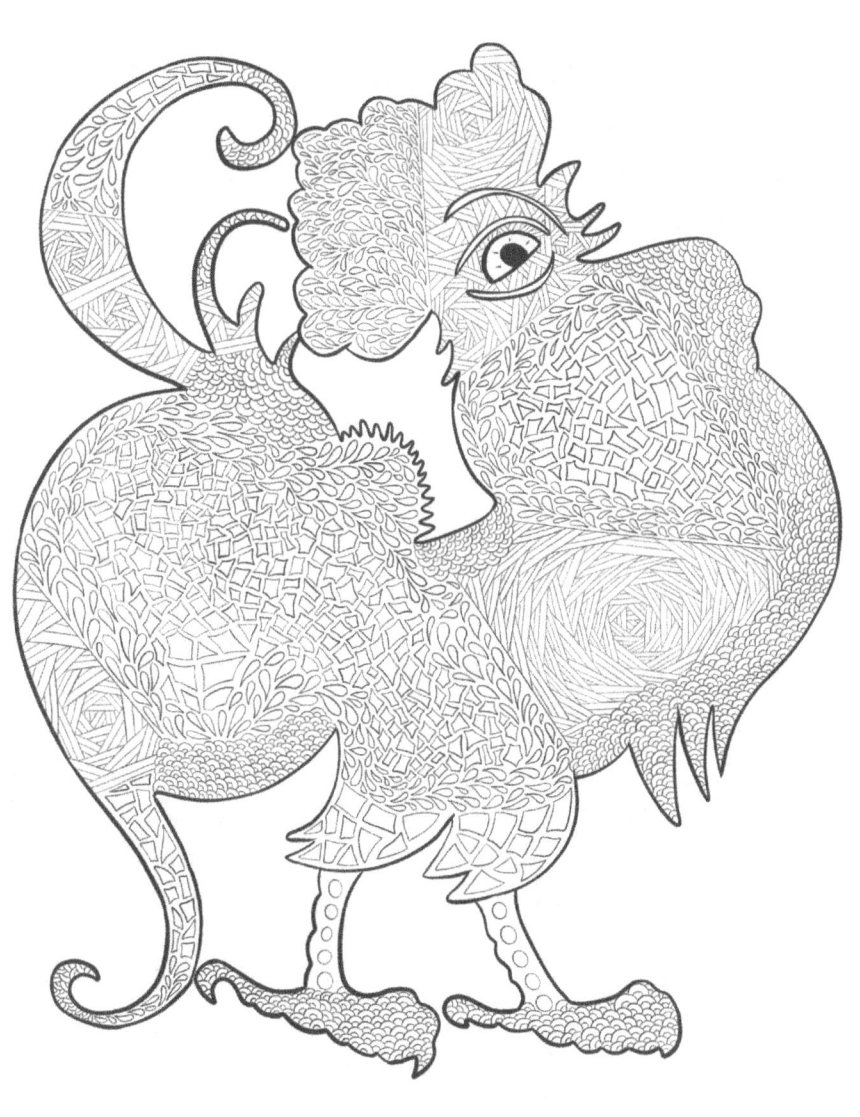

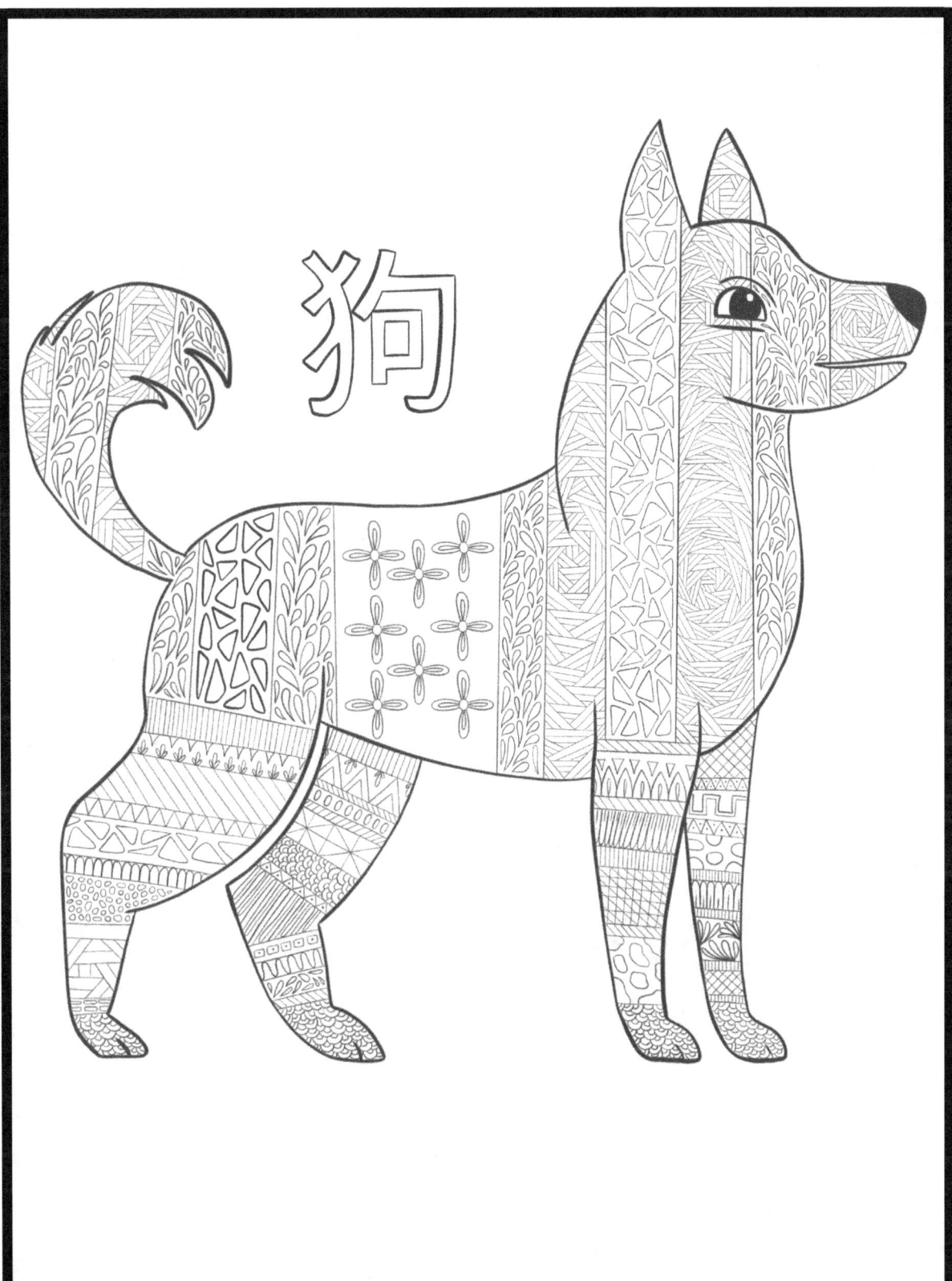

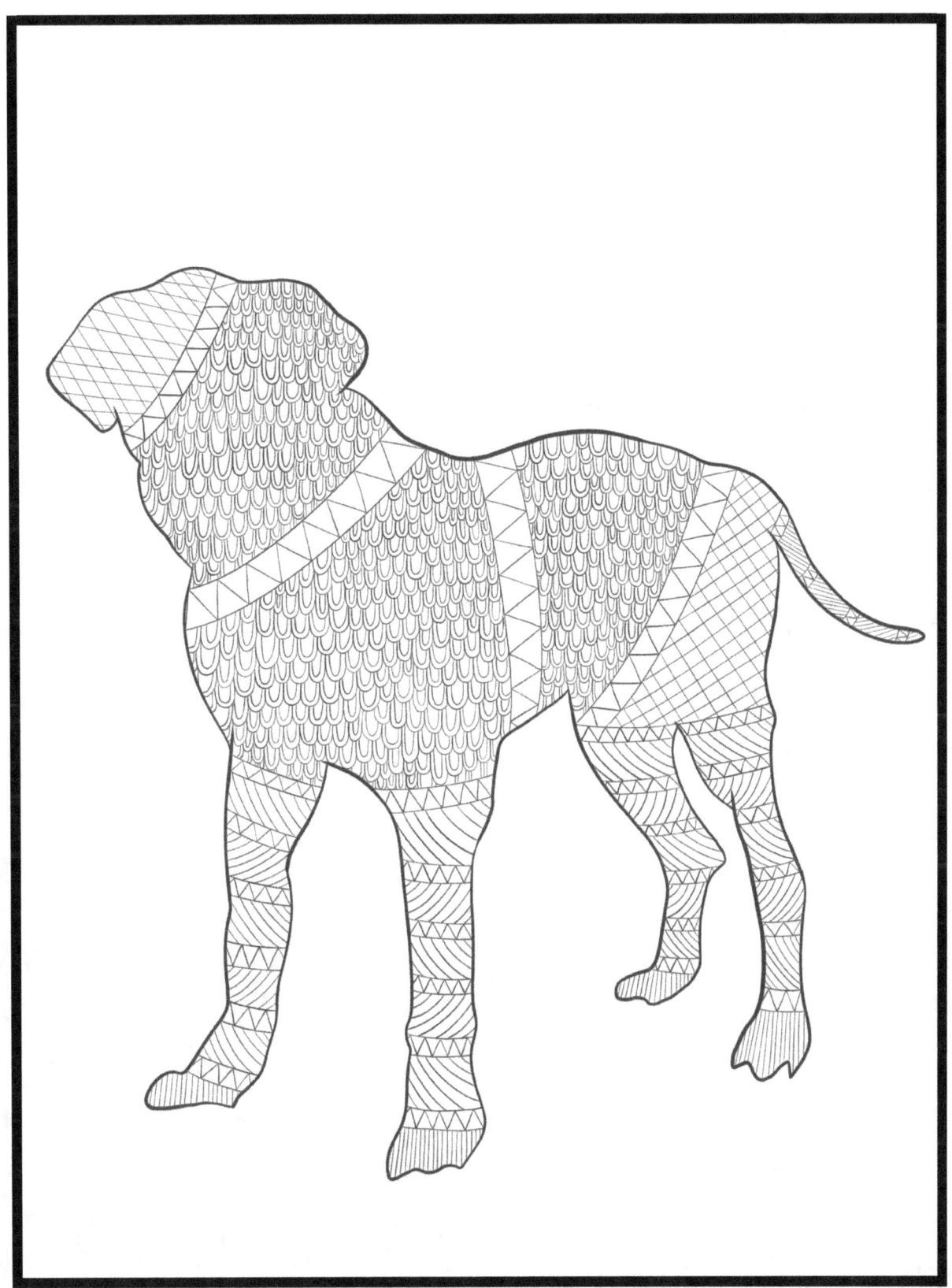

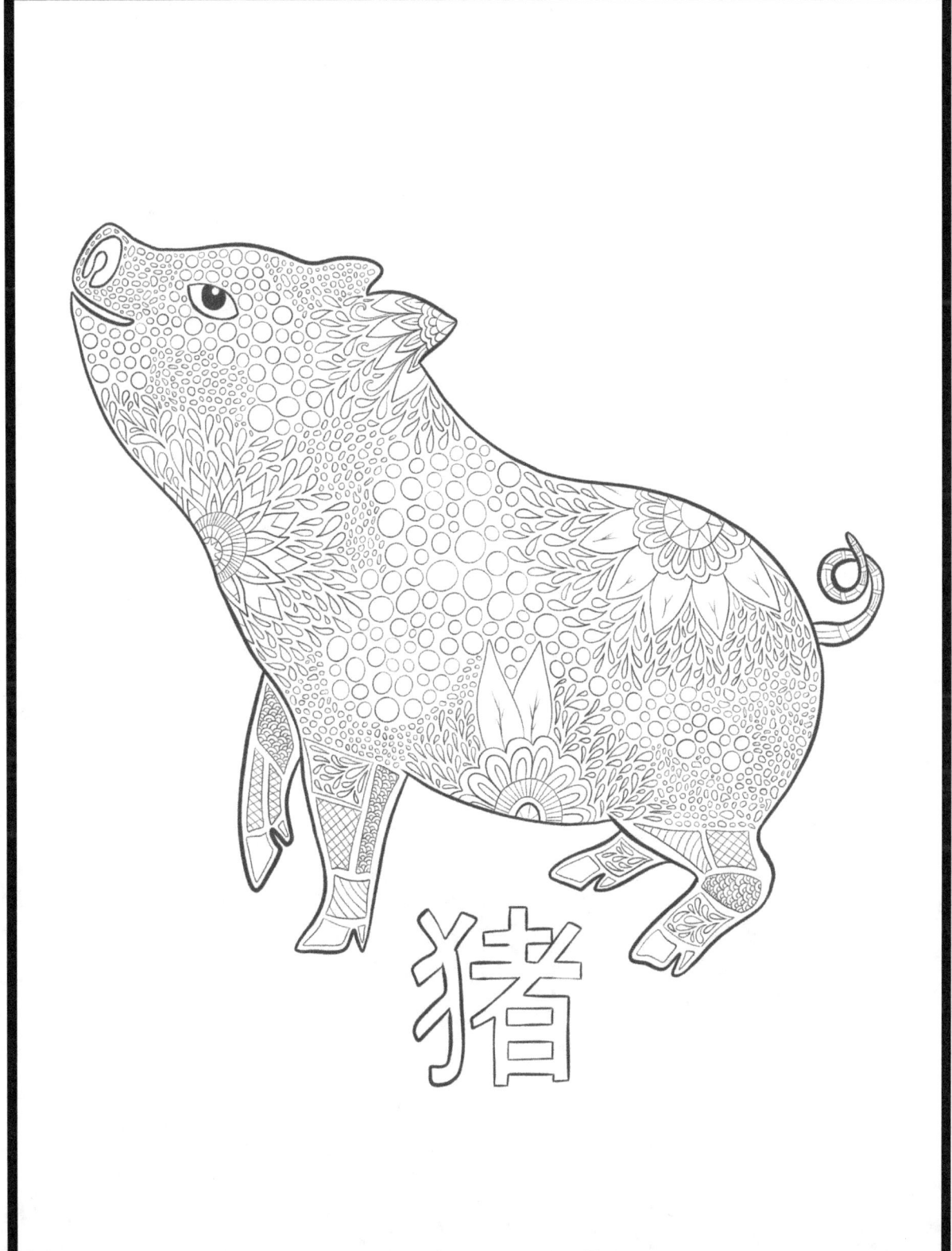

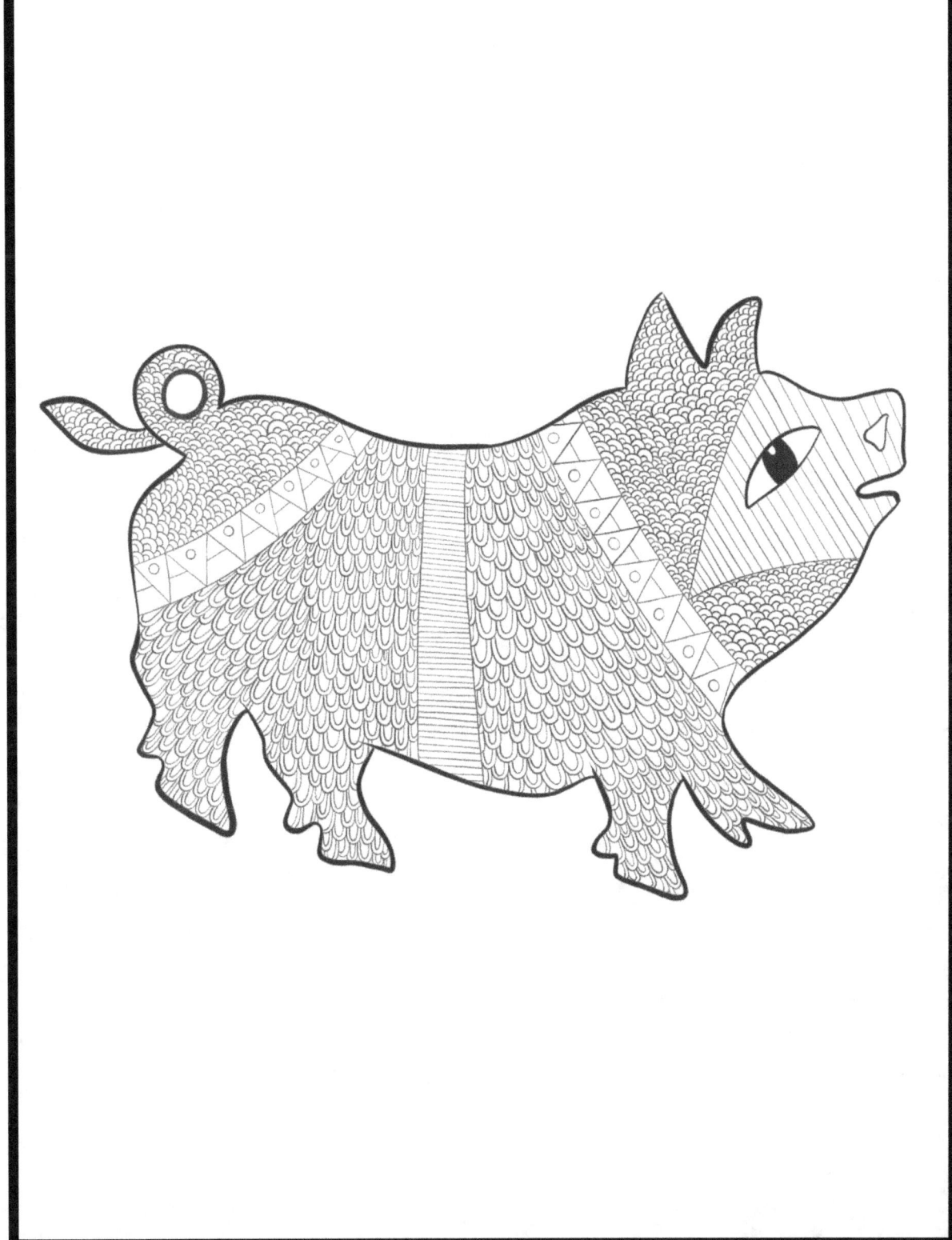

CHINESE ZODIAC SIGN

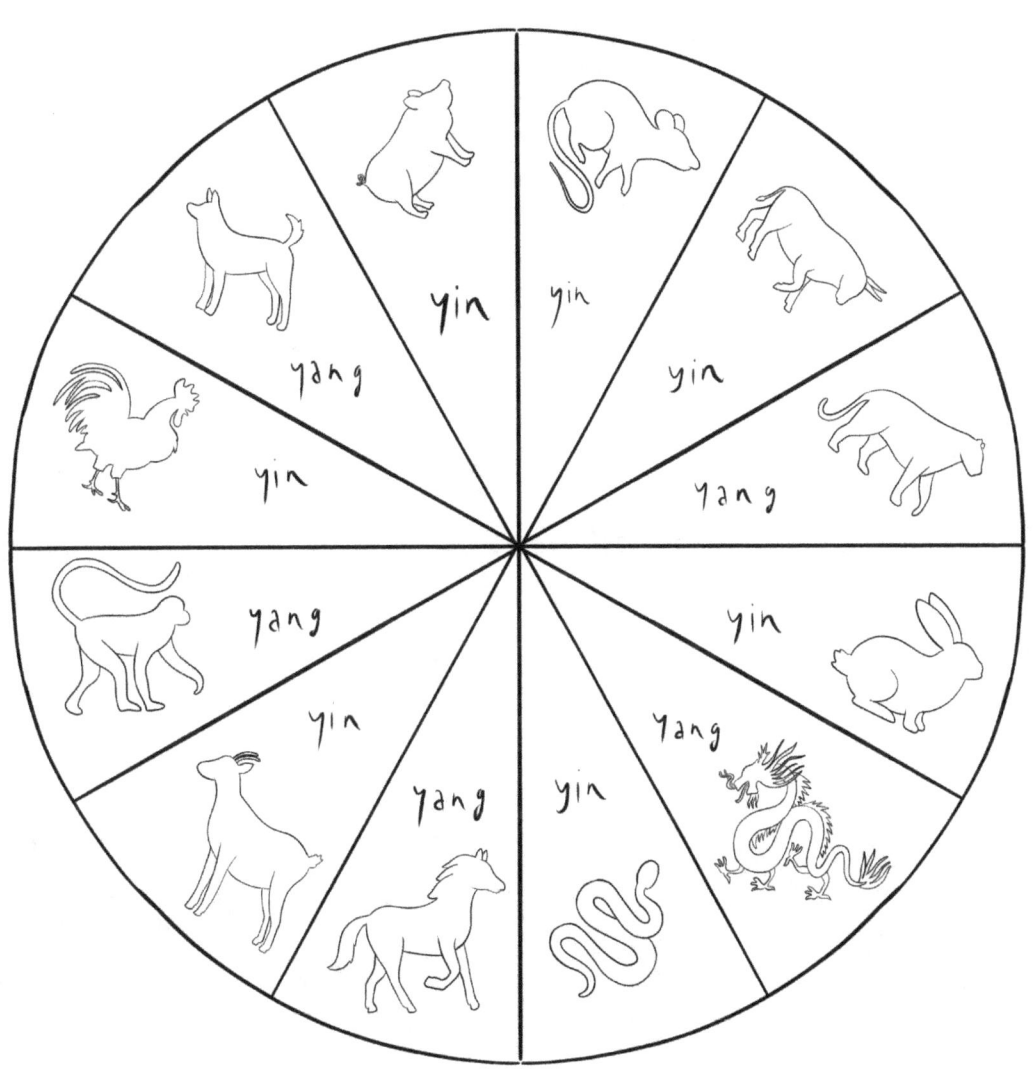

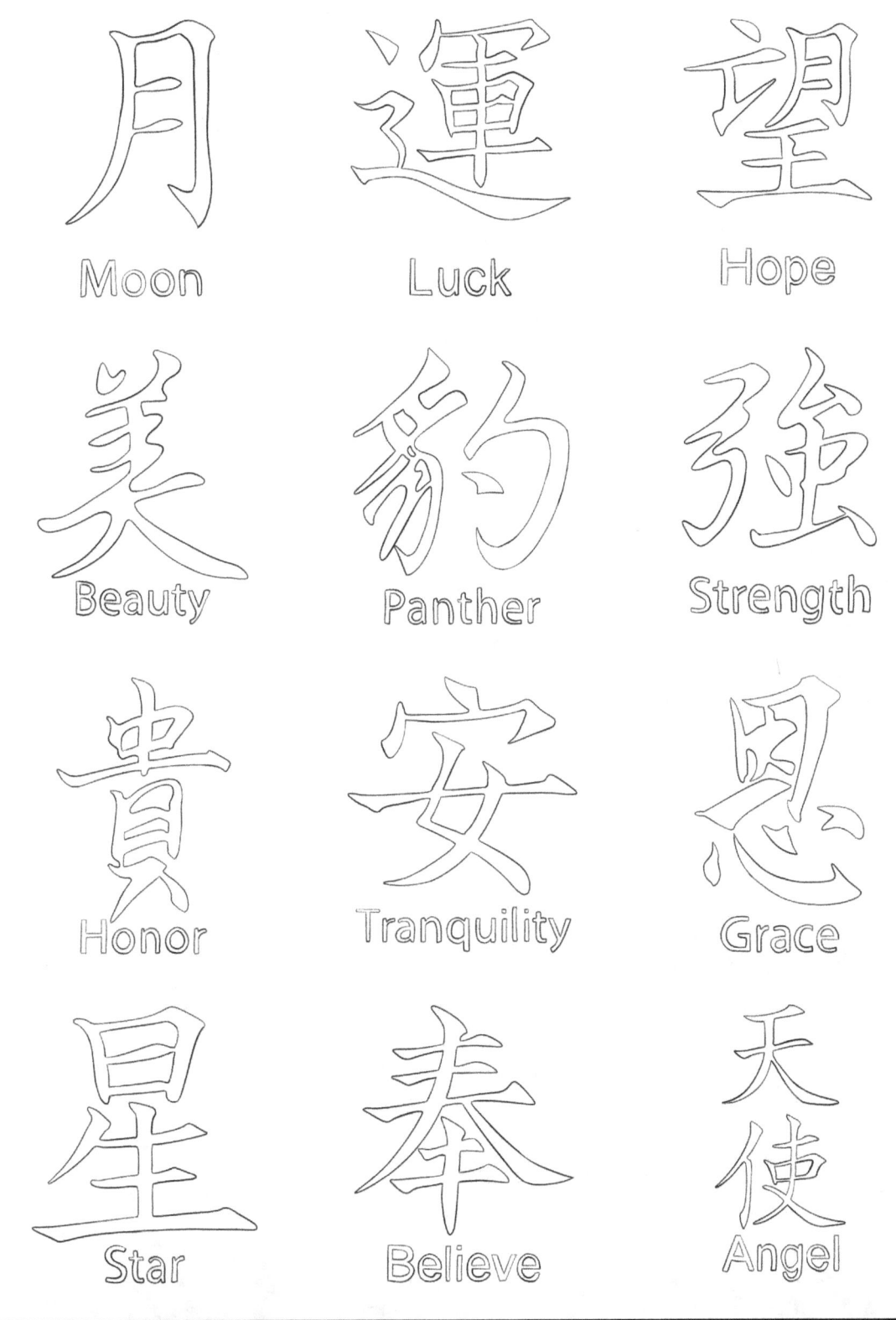

月 Moon

運 Luck

望 Hope

美 Beauty

豹 Panther

強 Strength

貴 Honor

安 Tranquility

恩 Grace

星 Star

奉 Believe

天使 Angel

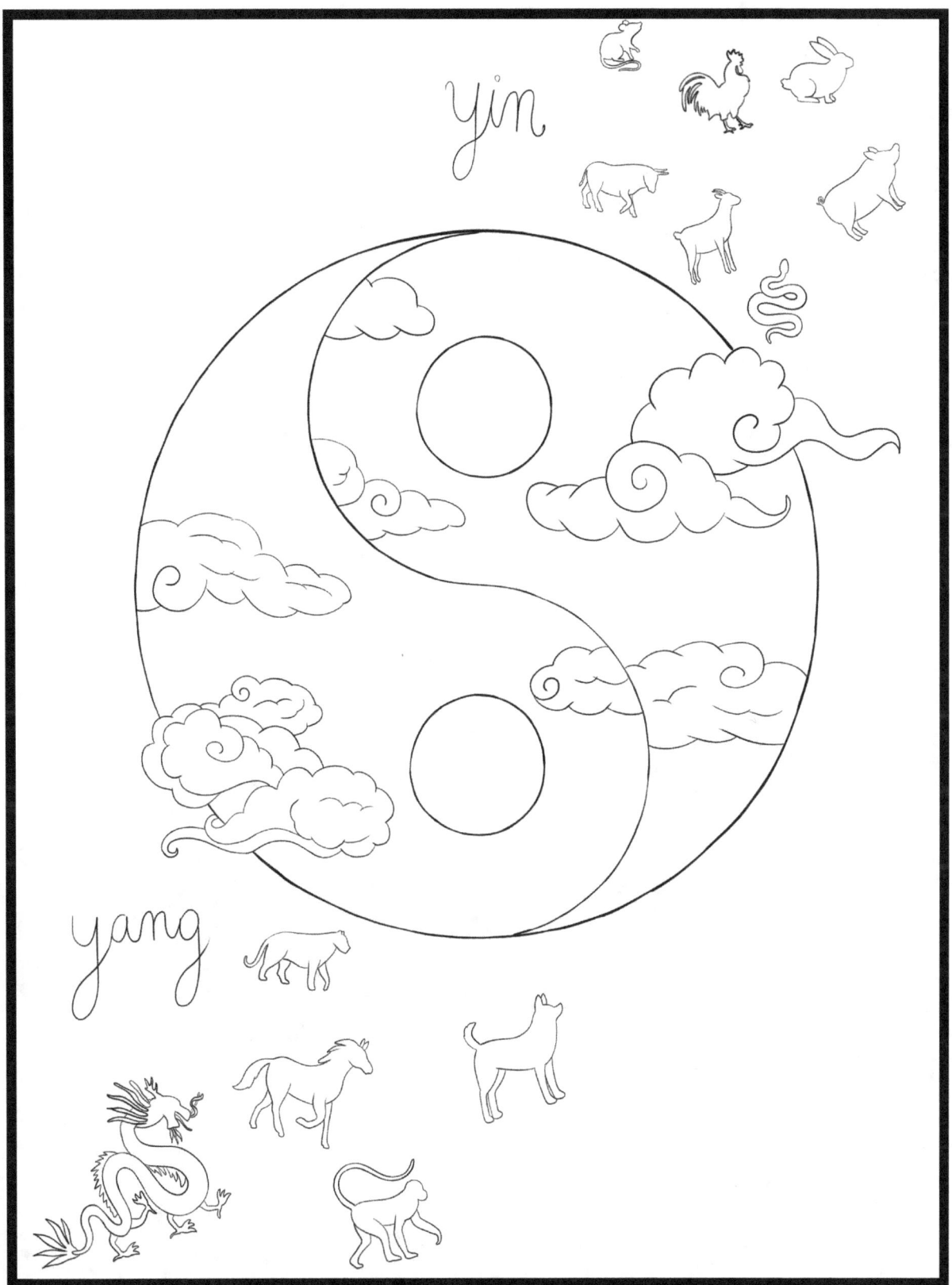

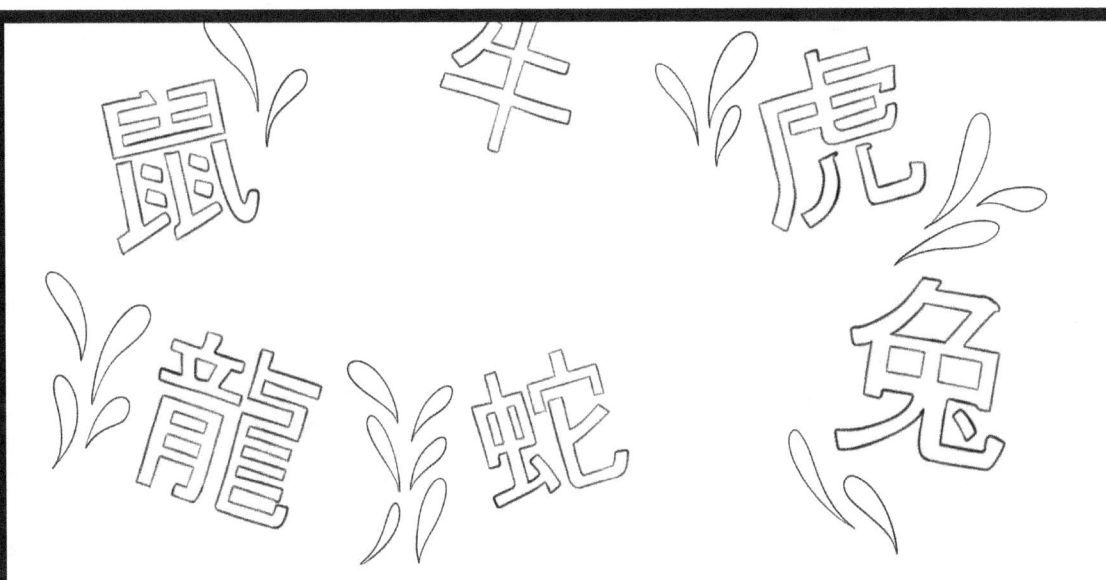

The End
You have reached the end of this adventure. I hope that you
enjoyed this coloring book. Share with us all your creativity coloring
on the social media : #llbdeco or @llbdeco.
Hope to see you again in the next book :)

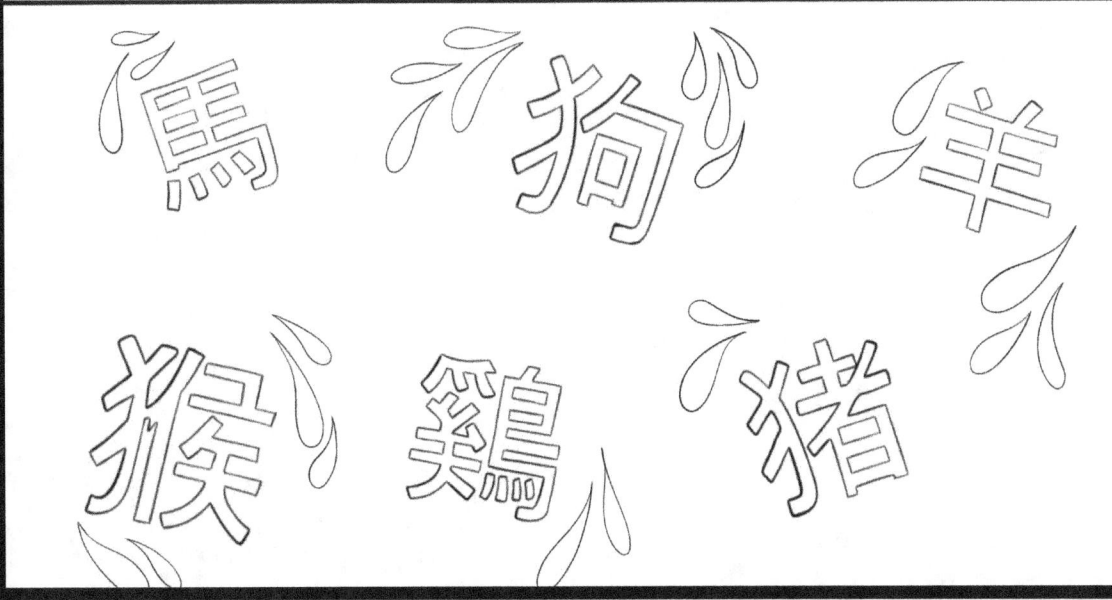